Amazon FBA E-Commerce

Frank Darrell

Table of Content

CHAPTER 1: Introduction to Amazon FBA

It takes a lot to run an e-commerce business. Let us say you are an entrepreneur selling high-end quality sports gears that you find in on clearance at a sporting goods store. Or maybe you are a retailer with a team that distributes high-quality products from your stores. Perhaps you are a large-scale product manufacturer, and you have to deal with large orders daily. Regardless of the size of products or services you distribute or how you obtain them, you have a lot to offer to the market. The situation calls for a way to develop your product. You are required to optimize your online marketing and advertising programs. In simple terms, you need to manage your business correctly.

The bulk in capacity and time required for management renders you unable to handle the tasks at once. Being a single being, you are incapable of moving the goods, branding, packing, and shipping individual orders and serve customer services at the same time. Whether you already sell through Amazon or may have been considering starting selling by Amazon, the right solution for your business is fulfillment by Amazon (FBA).

Amazon FBA has increasingly been the chosen selling platform for many business owners. The platform is by far the most popular way of earning an income online. Almost everyone can list an item on Amazon for sale. Whether the good is sourced through wholesale acquisition, manufactured by an individual, or is simply an old product that you no longer use. If you decide to enroll in the Amazon FBA program, you get the chance to automate order fulfillment by enjoying advanced distribution channels and fulfillment by Amazon. The services guarantee an income through an improved volume of sales from the coveted clients of Amazon. Statistics have shown that almost 33.33% of total sales on Amazon are from third-party sellers. The same study indicates that out of the top-ranked ten thousand sellers on Amazon, more than a third of them use the Amazon FBA platform.

Amazon FBA provides the platform for businesses to assemble products before millions of possible buyers regardless of the size of the companies. The services allow businesses to take advantage of the vast fulfillment network around the globe to boost their sales online. Additionally, FBA will enable enterprises to control their prime customer service and packing facilities. The truth of the matter is that Amazon is a leading company in the world, and customers tend to trust you if the giant company backs you. For that reason, Amazon FBA offers a great way to improve sales volume and enhance the brands of business across the world. In general, Amazon relieves you the majority of loads by handling such services for you. The most exciting part is the seamless incorporation of Amazon FBA with BigCommerce. The common platforms allow you to sell on both while Amazon handles fulfillment and manages inventory for your business.

What is Amazon FBA?

FBA stands for fulfillment by Amazon. The service falls among the two integral fulfillment options available for sellers on Amazon. The other fulfillment option provided by Amazon is fulfillment by merchants (FBM). FBM is a system that allows the seller to take care of packing and shipping orders as they come directly from clients. On the contrary, FBA will enable sellers to use Amazon as a stage to reach more customers and markets while Amazon ships the sold products. In general terms, Amazon sums up FBA by, "you sell it; we ship it." The FBA network is one of the notable giants that influence retail domination of the commerce sector by Amazon. The concept is based on the reality that Amazon sells billions of products worldwide, hence the need to ship the items to the buyers.

The FBA network has solved one of the long-standing problems in the eCommerce industry; how to ship sold products in an effective, efficient, simple, and fast way. As a business, retailer, or wholesaler, you face the initial challenge in reaching the global market. Many buyers do not like waiting longer for their shipment or incurring additional costs of conveyancing. If your business lacks a preplanned proper conveyance solution, you risk losing out to competitors and reducing the volumes of your sales. That is where Amazon FBA comes in handy. A plus about the Amazon FBA program is that you do not have to simulate the network; instead, you tap it in and let it work for you.

However, fulfillment b Amazon is not a free service. That calls for an answer to the question, is Amazon FBA worth a try? The focus is thus drawn on the advantages of FBA weighed against the disadvantages. For third-party sellers, the resounding answer to the questions is yes. As for the rest, the benefits accrued from the use of FBA may not justify the cost involved.

To spare you the headache of deciding the area to get involved, I will take you through Amazon fulfillment. What it is about, how much it costs to use, and many more. As discussed above, Amazon lets you sell while they handle the shipping for you. That is the general concept behind Amazon FBA. Simple and straight. However, the process involves a lot of steps that you need to take into consideration and get an insight into the same.

The Benefits of Using Amazon FBA

By enrolling in the Amazon FBA program, your business and clients are guaranteed a host of benefits and advantages that come along. You should know that Amazon has over 300 million active clients across the world. Out of the figures, 90 million are listed as prime customers in the United States of America alone. Brands that are available for these top customers are mostly availed through Amazon FBA.

Prime customers are found to spend a lot of money on averagely in purchases on Amazon compared to other regular customers. By statistics, a regular customer is estimated to spend $700 annually on purchases while a prime customer spends $1300 annually. The stats infer that if you are enrolled in Amazon FBA, your products are made visible to prime customers. This feature boosts sales as you enjoy a vast customer base. Benefits that you and your business will enjoy are:

Extensive and Cost-effective Shipping Options

As a business, if you have ever tried shipping products on your own, then you are familiar with the struggles. The process is not only time consuming but also tedious. Increased volumes of sales mean that you will have to spend a lot of time packing, shipping, and spending additional money in the process. Amazon FBA allows you and your business to offer more fascinating conveyance options to your clientele. The products you offer are eligible for free two-day shipping for Prime customers while most products are given free shipping offers. The cost of shipping through FBA is reduced compared to distributing the items on your own. Amazon has many contracts with shipping carriers that offer conveyance services at discounted rates. The discounts are passed to sellers. The considerable incentive guarantees massive sales translating into increased income.

Access to Customer Support and Management

Amazon offers both the business and your customers' free access to customer care services. The same applies to manage revenues. The process is hassle-free from your side and your customers'. Amazon is highly reputable in offering quality customer care services around the clock through phone, online chats, and emails. The excellent facilities are passed to FBA sellers with ease. Managing returns can be a tiresome process for most business owners. The challenges of dealing with unsatisfied clienteles, assessing revenues, and taking care of administrative functions are made lighter by Amazon. The company takes care of all inquiries, return conveyance labels, and reverse logistics. All this is done at a cost-effective charge.

Adaptability and Flexibility

The services offered through Amazon FBA are flexible to scale with your business regardless of size or sector. There are no set minimums for using the services in terms of costs. The scalability allows you to launch your business, to grow over time, and operate the business without demanding capital budgeting. Instead of concentrating so much on the business logistics, FBA offers you a chance to focus on the essential operations of the market, like running the product and brand lines.

Amazon FBA is also flexible in the sense that it can be incorporated with other channels such as Big Commerce and eCommerce to stores like eBay and Etsy. The possibility offers your business a multi-channel operation base.

Cost-effective Solutions

The Amazon pricing model is based on the sales and storage of your products. The system offers value-based payment, which ensures that you are not overcharged for services rendered to your business. The model is cost-effective and straightforward. Features of the products you list for sale are weighed against the price you pay. You can use the Amazon FBA fees calculator to make estimations of the fees that you are supposed to pay. Alternatively, you can get your hands on the FBA fees structures and referral commissions online through sites like DataHawk.com

Possibilities to Go Global

The Amazon FBA allows you to sell your products globally. For businesses based in the United States of America, your customers are allowed to visit your search, browse the goods, and get products that are eligible for exportation through the Amazon global selling program. The same application will enable you to sell directly to Canada and Mexico. For businesses in Europe, you are allowed to control the markets across Europe like the United Kingdom, Poland, the Netherlands, and Spain.

Vast Storage Capacities

The use of Amazon FBA saves you the worry of how much storage space you require for your products. No go down payments or tussle for storage facilities. The program offers flexible rates that make it easy to list any amount and size of products. You can store even a single product. The program also provides extensive storage facilities for sellers whose products have high inventory performance.

One Time Delivery

Amazon has numerous fulfillment centers across the globe. The vast networks make it easy to distribute products around every corner of the world as soon as clients place an order. Amazon can reliably deliver your products where your customers want them. Delivery takes a few days. Once your clients place an order, Amazon determines the closest fulfillment center to the customer and transports the ordered products from there.

Disadvantages of Using Amazon FBA

It is evident that anything with merit also exhibits some demerits. Amazon is no different. Even though the platform offers credible selling options, there exist a few flaws that a potential business owner should know.

FBA Is Not Free

The system is handy for businesses, sellers, and buyers alike. However, it is worth noting that the services are not offered at an open rate. Amazon applies storage fees and the cost of fulfillment. Someone looking forward to venturing in Amazon FBA eCommerce should be aware of the pricing policy. The best way is evaluating the fluidity of your products. If your inventory is likely to sell fast, then you can save on most costs associated with storage. The same applies to determine the profit margin for your products. If the products have a slim profit margin, it is not advisable to use Amazon FBA. The reason behind this is that you may end up paying fulfillment fees leading to ultimate loss.

Accumulating Storage Fees

Amazon offers affordable storage facilities. The fees charged are cost-effective. However, these changes when your inventory sits in the store for a long time without selling. Amazon s selling platform, not a storage facility. This means that the company will charge you more if your products are not selling. The accumulation of storage fees can reach a high limit leading to eventual loss on our part as a businessperson. Hint: go for fast selling products.

The Process of Preparing Your Products Can Be Complicated

Amazon provides strict guidelines on the preparation of products for shipment and sale. Products must be labeled correctly, the details entered into the Amazon database in the right formats, and conveyed to the correct hayloft. The processes involved in doing all this can be complicated, especially to first time sellers.

Keeping Track of Your Products Can Prove Challenging

Keeping records of your inventory can be very difficult. It is hard to stay on top of the available stock, how to restock. It equally not easy to know the products that are not selling since they are always out of sight. If you are a seller who utilizes multiple channels, syncing products is made more difficult.

Staying Up to Date on Sales Tax Is Very Difficult

Every country has varying tax regulations. The same applies to the different states in the United States. Keeping track of sales tax is only simple if your products are operated within a single country. Contrary to that, Amazon has several fulfillment centers in almost every state in the US. Furthermore, products are trundled between the many warehouses continually. It is, therefore, not easy to understand if you are supposed to collect sales tax for the state that your business is located or in every state that Amazon has an operational base.

Pooling Products Can Be Risky

Amazon offers the chance to pool your products with those from other sellers as long as they are in the same line. This program is meant to save labeling and prepping time. The problem with this arrangement is that some gets merchants can pool their counterfeit products with your authentic ones. The result may lead to negative reviews or even ban from Amazon selling platforms.

Getting Started: How to Create an Amazon FBA Account

The fulfillment by Amazon FBA business model has continued to absorb more sellers in the market environment who wish to expand their businesses to eCommerce. The model is no different from the conventional eCommerce business. However, Amazon has put in more innovative measures over the years to ensure that FBA becomes a leading player in the eCommerce business sector.

The fundamental aspects that underlie the model have seen more people trying their hands on the profitable, easy to use, and cost-productive venture. Instead of owners having to fulfill clientele orders one by one, Amazon comes into play to ensure that storage, packing, and shipping duties are got off your shoulders.

The outcome has seen many people venture into other fundamental aspects of the business without having to worry about logistics and so forth. With private labeling offers available, the eCommerce business model that has been put in place by Amazon allows you to improve the appeal of your brand. Sellers can thereby increase the volumes of sales and, consequently, the market value of the business. The description of Amazon FBA sounds appealing and may attract many upcoming and established entrepreneurs. If you are raring to go, this section provides the basic guidelines for getting started.

The FBA allows entrepreneurs to utilize Amazon's robust shipping linkages and vast market knowledge. As noted in the opening sections of this book, Amazon reduces the load of shipping, warehousing, and provision of customer services from the owners of the listed products. This means that entrepreneurs can identify with the market as big franchises without even being in the position. The sole focus of the impresarios is thereby to research product features that would enable quick sales while Amazon does the rest of the work. A typical eCommerce business model requires owners to figure out the logistics involved with moving their products in the market to reach potential customers in a good time. The lid has been lifted by fulfillment by Amazon, which does most of this work on your behalf.

What most people find challenging in an eCommerce business model is the process of inventorying added products for sale. However, the FBA prototype allows you only to ship your inventory to Amazon warehouses and let them take over the rest of the operations from there. The process of setting up your business, however, requires some step by step analysis and guides to ensure that you are eligible to get started. Below are the guidelines for getting started in fulfillment by Amazon.

Creating an Amazon Seller Account

Now that you are adequately warmed up and raring to venture in this business with potentially high income, we need to get your FBA business up and running. There are possibly seven steps that you need to follow to set up your FBA business fully. The seven steps are laden with tips and advice to ensure that you on not miss a hint while venturing in this fantastic opportunity.

Step One: Create an Account

First things first. To get your Amazon FBA business fully set up and running, you are required to follow some step by step filling of relevant information. This means that you cannot start an Amazon FBA business without an account. In theory, you can save this step and do it on a later date; however, it is advisable to complete the process if you are into the idea. The process initiated is creating an Amazon seller account. Setting up the account is very easy and requires some necessary information about the seller and the products to be listed.

The first step in creating the account is visiting the Amazon website. Once on the site, you need to scroll down the page up to a footer labeled "make money with us" click the link that is marked "Sell on Amazon." Reaching this point, you are halfway to go. Before you dive into the venture headfirst, some guidelines are recommended for sellers to follow before formalizing the process of registering an account.

The guidelines are mostly on paper works that are involved in the registration process of opening an account to start selling on Amazon FBA. Before proceeding to full registration, an individual is required to provide some information relating to the person and the business e, or she intends to start and run. The list below is some of the information needed to be filled in during the process.

1. Business Information

This section requires the seller to provide all the information relating to the business. Here, you will have to indicate the legal name of the venture, the address of the company, and the contacts that can be used to access the business for inquiries.

2. Email Address

It is necessary to indicate an email address that will be used for the business account. The email address should be up and running since it is the contact that will be used for most business communications. Essential updates from Amazon are sent through this email. Additionally, once the business is up and running, you will need to set up email subscriptions for your clients as a way of promoting your products. This is discussed later in the book.

3. Credit Card

For registration to proceed, you need an internationally accepted credit card with a valid address for billings. The credit card is used to make most of your payments and is an essential trading tool in the Amazon FBA business model.

4. Phone Number

You must provide a phone number that can be used to each for urgency. The number is also required to complete the registration process before your seller account is made active.

5. Tax ID

One of the requirements for registration o Amazon FBA seller business account is valid information about your tax identity. The tax ID includes your social security number and information as well as the federal tax identification number of the business. In cases where you do not have the tax ID information, the registration process will be delayed to conduct a "1099-K Tax Document Interview."

6. State Tax ID

Apart from the federal tax ID number, you are also required to provide a state tax ID. This ID is more of tax information for the state in which the business operates. State tax information can be challenging since you may work in more than one state, yet different states have their tax regulations. However, you may have some relief since the US Supreme Court (2018) overturned the rules about tax responsibilities that eCommerce traders have when making online sales.

In cases where you fail to understand or interpret the tax regulations and requirements, it is advisable to seek the services of a tax advocate with specialization on online tax responsibilities. An example of such a service can be found through salestaxandmore.com.

Once you are through with the paperwork requirements, there are some aspects of the business that you need to understand first before proceeding to the next chapter. The set process gives you the option to sign up as an individual or a professional. The two fields are different in scope and charges that need to be explained and understood before proceeding.

Signing Up as Individual Vs. Signing Up as Professional

Once you are past the "Sell on Amazon" link, you are required to either choose setting up your business as an individual or an expert. Understanding the two is vital in making the upfront decision on which one to choose. Below is an elaboration of the two to help you understand each separately.

An individual account does not have a monthly subscription fee. The account is free.

However, various limitations come with setting up your business with an individual account. A professional account comes with a monthly subscription fee of $39.33. The account is, however, exempted from the first-month subscription, which is to means that you are not charged for the first month of setting up the account. The second and subsequent months attract the listed fee.

An individual account is recommended for people who are just trying to figure out the business model and how it operates. This is an account of experimentation and related stuff. On the other hand, if you are planning to grow your business over time and reach vast markets and customer base, you are advised to go for a professional account.

Picking the Right Products to Sell
Step Two: Identify Your Forte

This step has proven to be the most challenging of them all, especially for newcomers in the business model. The excitement of being able to sell online, sometimes cloud sellers' judgment making them want to sell almost everything that they can get their hands on. On the limitations of setting up an Amazon FBA business, I stressed that Amazon is a selling company, not a storage facility. I went further to elaborate that Amazon will charge you as a business if your products are not moving. You are therefore required to choose the right inventory for your business. You should select fast-moving products to cut the cost of storing them in Amazon warehouses. The best way of doing this is by carrying out a market survey. You should evaluate the products and try to determine how your brand will fit into the market. Here are tips to get you started.

Follow Your Passion

The best way to identifying your niche is by considering the area that you are most passionate about or like most. List down these areas and evaluate each, isolating others based on your metrics. Products in this line are most likely to go down well with you and your business. If you find it hard to come up with a list, think about your hobbies, things that you research most of the time, your line of expertise and professionalism, etc. You only need to figure out of the box to establish a brand that will move you and the market as well.

Brainstorm Products That Go with Your Passion

So, you have established an area that you want to specialize in your business. The second step is listing all products that are available in the areas that are in line with your passion. Write the products down corresponding to each range of your choice.

Narrow Down Your List

Once you have listed products that fall under the areas of your choice, you need to narrow down the list to a specific niche. For instance, if you have chosen clothing and designing as your area of expertise and have identified various products, you should come up with a more specific field as "baby wears."

Make the List Even Narrower

Baby wears can be an expansive area for starters. If you are not willing to go into the broad niche, you can come down even further by specializing in baby footwears only. By choosing the items and products in areas that you are passionate about, you will be curious to do more research. The practice makes you more knowledge, which in turn ensures that you create more elaborate product listing, blog post, advertisement copies, and many more.

Finding Suppliers/Wholesalers for Your Business
Step Three: Carry Out Market Research for Your Products

As popularly stated, this is the step where the rubber meets the road. You have come up with a list of products that you would wish to deal with and make the base of your business. However, offering the products, you have chosen to the consumers may turn out to be an entirely different outlook. You are required to carry out a survey and additional research of the products on your list. Well, unless you are ready to shut the business before it even starts. Below are some practical steps that will help you carry out the analysis of the products.

Overall Product Search

At this phase of product research, you are going to do a general search about the products on your list. The purpose of this study is getting better ideas of listed product distribution in the world and the features of the products. Additionally, the search gives you an overview of what to expect when dealing with the products you have on your list. To be more elaborate, you will have to the product on eCommerce sites and businesses. Conduct your search on Etsy, Amazon, and other leading online retail stores. Alternatively, you can google the products and analyze the search results. Take note of the online retail stores that handle the product. If the effects on other retail outlets point out prices between $10 and $50, then consider yourself safe. Online products that fall between those price ranges are mostly impulse buys. Impulse buys are useful in a way that you will be able to sale a large volume of goods.

Using Keyword Tools

For active product research, you have to use keyword tools such as jungle scout, Merchant Words, etc. these keyword tools are crucial in evaluating the demand patterns about the product of your choice. The purpose of using these tools to conduct ta product research is to see how often the products are included in keyword searches. This way, you can assess the probabilities of the outcomes being a good sale. Practically, demand and supply patterns in the market influence the purchase of products and services. Products on high demand tend to sell more at reasonable prices, depending on the availability of the products. If you can establish that the products you intend to sell on FBA are highly demanded, you may as well be on your way to potentially lucrative ventures. The rationale behind this notion is that your products should be in high demand while there are fewer suppliers in the market. The market gap created by the imbalance is sufficient for the growth of your business.

Best Seller Rankings (BSR)

The best-seller ranking by Amazon should not be at the top of your list when determining the best product to list in the market. However, you should use it to know the items and categories that are on high demand and attract many customers. Consider the first five best-ranked products on BSR that correspond to the products on your list. This category is always the easiest to break into the market. On the other hand, items with a lower BSR rank are the most selling products compared to competing products. If your products fall within this rank, brace up for a highly competitive venture.

Additional Tools for Market Research

Other tools can help you do product and market research. These tools provide a lot of data on goods and the market to help in an in-depth analysis of the same. Additionally, the devices provide metrics for the interpretation of the data available about the merchandise. The research tools include AMZ Scout and Base, Sonar, Watched Item, and Unicorn Smasher, among others.

Amazon FBA Fees

After you have carried out your research and narrowed down to the items that you intend to list in the market, you will need to consult Amazon on the costs associated with the items. Determining the fees charged for your products is essential in computing the profitability of the business. The costs levied on items vary depending on several features such as size, need for specialized storage or handling, among others. Always try to keep the related fees at the minimal to reduce your expenses and increase your profits.

Additional Product Research Tips

If you have followed the steps above diligently, you ought to have a trimmed list of products from our original first list. At this point, you are ready to move on to the next step. However, there are some things that you should be aware of if you are not particularly precise about the products that fit your business model, goals, and targets. Here are some tips to help you hack through.

Do not enroll in a category that has established products and widely recognized brands. Going against big players in the market may spell some doom for your business. Regardless of demand, people tend to buy products that are globally recognized. Avoid that area completely. These products are from people with better marketing strategies and large budget allocations that give them a competitive edge over yours.

Bulk and clearance products from retail and wholesale outlets are highly recommended. These products allow you to sell branded products, which help in growing your business in the long run. A point to note is that these products are available occasionally, so do not base your entire FBA business on them. They are only meant to help get your footing and supplement your business in the short term.

Go on a local scouting mission. You do not have to do your market research on online stores alone. You can also research local retail stores. Walk around to see what products are on the shelves, which products are fast selling, and which ones are lacking in the market. Alternatively, you can use barcode scanning apps to conduct the research.

By the time you have followed the above steps thoroughly and utilized the extra tips to do your product and market research and analysis, you should be ready to establish the products and items that you intend to list in the market.

Step Four: Establish Your Supplier

Establishing a product and the category you wish to deal with is half the task. To fully start listing items for sale, you will need to go through an additional step. That is establishing your product sourcing, where you will get the products regularly. Without a reliable supplier, you will not have the products to sell. This is, however, the most time consuming of all the steps and one that requires a lot of focus. You should establish a supplier who can get you the highest quality products and in time to meet the demands in the market. To get such a supplier, you need the following.

Test the Products

This step is crucial in determining the quality and effectiveness of what you intend to avail of to the market. Faulty products can lead to losses and even get you banned from using Amazon altogether. If you have interacted with the product in the past, then there is no need to test it. However, if you intend to offer generic products to cut costs, you will have to make sure that quality is not compromised and that your clients will be happy with what they get. Request for a sample from your supplier and test the product before getting them to the market for your clients. You have to make sure that your customers are satisfied and are offering value for their money if you intend to grow your business.

Find a Supplier

In most cases, people go for the most cost-effective suppliers. It advisable to always weigh the cost against quality before you settle for a broker. The list below will get you started in finding the right supplier for your products.

Foreign Suppliers

Many business owners using the Amazon FBA business model go for overseas suppliers such as Alibaba. These suppliers are known to offer products in bulk and at a lower cost compared to local retailers. The margin ensures that when you source your products from foreign suppliers, your profit ratios are increased. However, before you opt for international suppliers, be sure to consider the cost of conveying the products.

Local Trade Shows

Look out for local trade fairs and exhibitions with possible suppliers parading what they can offer your business. The trade shows often host big players in the given industries and can be an excellent place to establish your sourcing. You can also search for trade shows through the internet and leading trade magazines and journals.

Bulk and Clearance Items from Local Retailers

Bulk and clearance products from retail and wholesale outlets are highly recommended. These products allow you to sell branded products, which help in growing your business in the long run. A point to note is that these products are available occasionally, so do not base your entire FBA business on them. They are only meant to help get your footing and supplement your business in the short term.

Local Manufactures

If you are dealing with a product that is manufactured locally, make use of this opportunity to establish your product sourcing. The local producers will recognize your support for their products and offer you some discounts. Additionally, creating a good relationship with local manufacture can go a long way in ensuring that you are restocked on credit. To grow your business, you will require to input more products that are in line with the market niches. Creating a long-term, positive relationship with the local supplier will ensure that you do not fall short of options.

Conduct Shipment Research

As indicated above, reduced wholesale prices do not benefit the business if the cost of shipping the products is way above your budgets. Factoring the cost of shipping the products into your final budget is essential in determining the most effective supplier for your business. Overseas shipping involves many regulations, taxes, and international laws that must be applied. Always ensure that you weigh all factors and their effect on the final shipping cost before you opt for any foreign supplier.

Apart from the cost of the shipment process, other features are equally essential to be considered. The time taken to deliver the goods to you is very crucial, especially for fast selling products. You always need a continuous flow of goods to ensure that at no given time will experience a shortage. Fast selling products get out of stock fast, thus the need to have a supplier that will deliver the stocks quickly and continuously. Timely shipping is thereby an essential feature to consider when choosing the right supplier. State rules may also slow down the shipping process, always ensure that you stay current on the rules and plan before maintaining a good stock.

Ship Your Product

The next step after establishing your product sourcing is placing your first order and shipping the products. You can choose to send the products to yourself or have them shipped to Amazon warehouses. The latter is the more cost-effective of the two options. If you decide to have the goods shipped to Amazon fulfillment centers, then you have to follow the specified Amazon guidelines on how to prepare and ship inventories.

Chapter 2: Having the Right Mindset for FBA Business

In any given marketplace, the best-sellers are those who can understand their intentions for selling a particular product and how that benefits the clientele. The balance between the two results in a more natural sales process and customer experience. The question that arises in this process is how to create balance. In understanding this, sellers should take note of many factors, the most crucial being training. Even basic training can turn a novice into a completely super merchant. But in essence, we would like to know what sets the best FBA sellers apart from the rest of the pack. Well, this chapter answers in detailed explanation and steps; the mindset. How a salesperson identifies with the product and the general selling process is essential in determining the best salesperson. At the top of this analysis is the seller's ability to exhibit the right mindset and personal motivations towards the business.

Why FBA Sellers Need a Business Growth Mindset

For a successful venture on Amazon FBA business, sellers need to pull from the pool of average merchants by curating the right mindset for business growth. The ability to do so is what makes or breaks a seller. In this section, I am going to take a different approach from the how-to ABC approach and concentrate on the mindset. The reason for this chapter comes in the wake of sellers jumping into FBA businesses with the wrong mindset and ending up ditching the venture or being shut down.

In this chapter, I would like to identify two types of mindsets; a fixed mindset and a mindset set on growth. The difference between the two is that one focuses on a specific aspect regardless of changes, while the other focuses on a particular point with the mind on different elements and flexible enough to embrace new practices. Choosing the right mindset is key to a successful experience on Amazon FBA. The good thing about it is that all you have to do is choose.

It is, however, very reasonable to have a fixed mindset. This is not something we are taught in school. In fact, to some people, it is unconscious. So, it is not your fault if you are not up to speed on this fundamental idea. Worry not, I am here to assist you in developing the right approach and helping you succeed in your business.

We can all agree that the right mindset is more productive than a fixed one. FBA business has its challenges as pointed out in chapter one; however, with the right mindset, a seller is capable of navigating the drawbacks instead of putting blames on other factors.

The course of operating FBA business will poise a lot of challenges that will continuously test your mindset as a business person. It can be devastating if you react to such problems with a fixed mindset. Here is how you can cultivate the right mindset to help you turn your fortunes for the best.

Strive to Make Yourself Better

The first thing you need to do is to identify the skills required to start and run an Amazon FBA business. Gauge your skills against what is needed. Here is a list of what you need to know:

1. Good organization
2. Sales and marketing skills
3. Persuasion
4. Time management
5. Copywriting

Now that you know what it takes, you need to hone these skills to better your business. This way, you will find yourself above the majority of your peers. The skills cannot be developed overnight. It takes consistency and patience to cultivate and better them. For instance, let us look at sales and marketing skills. To market your products well to the extent that your sales flow regularly and continuously, you need to develop a good advertisement campaign, say pay per click. The process is more than just learning how it works. You need to completely master how to set up the drive, solicit clients, and market your product thoroughly.

All this is just marketing within the Amazon FBA program, which is very easy to master and set up. Alternatively, you can make use of Facebook Ads. This platform can be significant when ranking the performance of your products on Amazon. The best part is that Facebook Ads can be linked to Messenger Bots. Once this is done, you can deliver a certain percentage off token automatically through the two platforms. The messenger bot enables you to build a list of potential customers.

I have shown you how to create an email subscription list. Just a recap, you invite your clients to leave an email address that can be used to give them updates and notifications about the product or a new product altogether. Alternatively, you offer clients a gift in exchange for their email subscription. A messenger bot is slightly different, and the system gets people to subscribe to your bot by merely reacting to your Facebook Ads and posts.

Have you noticed how off topic I am at this point? Does it blend well with you? Well, that is the point here. If you are okay to learn a new marketing strategy (messenger bots), you have a business growth mindset. If you have noticed that I am getting off-topic and don't like the idea, your mindset is fixed. A fixed mindset expects me to be in line with the theme. A slight deviation and you are all up in arms. This way, you do not consider something new that can promote your business knowledge, and by choosing not to learn, you are deciding to wade through murkier water. By considering this idea, you get your business in a better position than your competitors, and this is just one skill. Imagine learning a new skill every day.

Expectations

By the end of this book, you will find it easy to identify the right product to list, getting a supplier, and shipping them to Amazon storage facilities. The hardest part comes in ranking your products, making sales, and marketing your brand. Amazon is the largest marketplace, and it attracts many sellers. This makes the competition very intense, and without learning new skills, you will find yourself falling behind and swimming among the average sellers who complain about how hard selling on Amazon is.

The skills listed above will take you time to master. And even after learning them, you will still need time to improve each. It is a continuous process. The process makes you a successful person, not just in FBA business but in every aspect of your life. The tactics of survival in Amazon needs you to change accordingly and cultivate a business growth mindset to get ahead of the average seller.

The approach may be different from the usual how-to, but the content is equally important. Knowing how to do something is as important as tuning your mindset on learning it. That is what makes the difference between an ordinary seller and a business-minded seller. FBA business, just like any other eCommerce business, will attract a lot of challenges. Without the right mindset, you will find these challenges frustrating. We can agree on one thing that once your business starts to frustrate you; the outcome will never be positive.

As much as some challenges may be hard to navigate, the right mindset sets the records straight that you have to do whatever it takes to get yourself back on track. You have to be better and a stronger version of yourself to get it done. And when you are faced with a similar problem in the future, you will be in a better position to handle it effectively and as fast as possible.

For a new seller or a beginner, hoping to start an Amazon FBA business, selling your listed items on Amazon can be a perfect idea. If done right, you may end up freeing yourself from a lot of financial crises and at the same time find time to spend with your family and friends. On the contrary, it can also leave you very broke and hopeless, if not done correctly. This spells why adequate preparation is critical whenever you plan to start a business.

How to Get Prepared

The easiest way to getting prepared for a business venture is by researching YouTube videos, reading blog posts from established sellers, and many other primary sources of information. The trick works for a lot of people. However, some might find it not so easy due to the lack of direct personal assistance. To navigate this challenge, new sellers require an established expert in the field. There are two ways of getting this aid.

1. Investing in a Course

An educative course is a very effective way of getting started because it lays a step by step tutorial of the entire process. A seller can enroll in an online class to greater success. Udemy offers such online tutorials that can help build your knowledge and mindset. Such lessons can save you a lot of time, which an essential factor in your business. However, you should note that learning from books may be different from applying the knowledge practically.

2. Investing in a Coach/Mentor

A mentor, unlike a course, can guide you through the practical parts and help you avoid costly mistakes. This means you will find someone who is already in the business to hold your hands. They know what it takes to start an Amazon FBA business. They have experienced challenges and know how to mitigate risks. They have the best practices at their fingertips. These are people who can get a solution to your problems and guide you in the right direction. Borrowing a leaf from them will be beneficial.

This book is designed for both the course and the coach. It offers you a step by step guides on how's and directs your mindset towards the same. Additionally, the subsequent chapters will answer your questions on getting started and running the FBA business.

For beginners, the sole focus on starting an Amazon FBA business is always laid on the money part, seemingly, the six or seven-figure screenshots, fancy cars, and the dollar signs. However, very few to realize that an entrepreneurial business mindset is what gets you to that point in life. The opportunity to start small and expand seems impressive, and considering the many people who have made it in FBA business, you will tend to confide in yourself that you can too.

That is an excellent start. The confidence and self-belief that you, too, can sail with the elite and compete with the established FBA merchants is a positive point to start from. It is all okay, but many processes involved will narrow you down to one aspect of life; the mind. When the mind is positive, so will the results. You may not be a firm believer in pep talks, but at some point, in life, you have probably come across or experienced something coming to pass due to the determination of the doer. To succeed, you will need to develop a positive mindset. This is how you can do it.

How to Develop the Right Mindset

In this section, I will provide tips to help you hone the business mindset that is suitable for a successful FBA business. The eight simple steps provided below are meant to give your mindset a boost.

Defining Your Success

Defining what success is to you is very crucial in establishing a good business. Many people dive into business to make money, but the lack is limited in purpose. They are fine as long as they can get a penny from their sales even if the business is not making notable progress. This is an average seller, and such a person lacks a destination. They cannot define where they want to be five years from now. Is that why you wake up every morning?

The same point should be applied to the FBA business. You should have a clear purpose. Visualize where you want your business to be in the future. Ask yourself what you can get from the store. Do you want the company to build a legacy for you? Do you want the business to get you a dream car? It is by knowing what you want that you can implement a process to achieve it. Once you have identified the purpose of the business, you will work down your sleeves to hit the target.

The next step is estimating the figures. Draw your profit projections. Either monthly or annually, you need to come up with a profit margin that you would like to form your FBA business. This aspect is critical in scaling down and identifying the best products for the same. In summary, when defining your success, I would want you to think of business success as a continuous process rather than an event.

Creating Success Through Consistency

The little steps you have identified to make your first sale on Amazon can translate into a thousand sales if you practice working hard in a disciplined and consistent manner. If anything is to go by, sweat yourself out to the extent that you don't think about the processes or the effort and resources you invest to succeed. Make it a habit, be it waking up at 2 am to conduct new product research or driving for hours to meet some clients or a supplier. Think about the target rather than the process of getting there.

On the other hand, you don't have to be so hard on yourself. Always give yourself a break. That is why you chose to invest in your FBA business; to get yourself some freedom. Having the drive to do things in a significant way is incredible, but it won't count if you drown yourself too much into it that you end up losing your heart or mind along the way. Reward yourself with some timeout and rest. You are not a robot, and the right mindset does not mean that you have to whip yourself until you get where you want to be.

Separate Your Emotions and Judgment from the Business

At times you will find some processes and activities in your Amazon FBA business very dull. For instance, I find dealing with annual tax returns and revenue computation sucking. This is not the only case that can get you on the low. Seeing your merchandise move slow despite the effort and resources you have invested in them can be frustrating at times. However, you don't have to put your emotions ahead of the necessary tasks. Trust the system you have implemented and moved on diligently.

You can get it from your mentor that they had to pass through the same problems to get where they are. Or sometimes you find out that you messed along the way. The best thing to do is to correct the mistakes and move on with the business.

Mistakes are Meant to Better You

Every time you make a mistake, remember to dust yourself off and continue with the journey. Do more extensive research for the next inventory. Invest more resources than before. Spend time analyzing your competitors. Create a better listing. Market your brand more and raise your quality. That is the ultimate resolution of the right FBA business mindset.

Why this resolve? It is proven that doing the same thing a thousand times gets you a thousand times better than you were initially. You end getting to the point that you may find yourself creating a new product from what you initially deemed perfect. As an Amazon FBA seller, you will grow with experience, and the little failures will improve your success possibilities. Your mind and body always need to be rewired.

Look at It as an Investment, Not a Cost

Everything that you throw into the business should be considered as an investment, not a cost of operation. Be it the dollars, the time, the research, or any other effort, and it is well invested. Whether it reaps benefits (profit) or ends up going through the drains. Whether it becomes a valuable business asset or a life lesson. Whatever is meant to improve the business is right for you. Do not look at how bad it turned. That is why I started by showing how mistakes are essential. So, the next time you think of throwing in some extra XYZ, think of it as value-added, not cost incurred.

Working Hard Is Good, Working Smart Is Better

Sweating through the processes to get your business where it needs to be is okay. At the same time, you need to consider the importance of automation and innovative ways to apply technology into the system. Technology can be a significant contributor to the success of your eCommerce business and at the same time, turn your Amazon FBA business experience into the most pleasant lifestyle driver. So, consider working hard, but also embrace technology where applicable.

Spread Your Wings Further

The last aspect that you need to take into consideration is expanding your FBA business. And as they say, do not put all your eggs in one basket. There is no marketplace without risks. The only sure way of mitigating risks that may threaten the ability of your business to sustain itself by diversifying. Be it a new product that you want to introduce, or improve an existing product, or discover additional marketplaces, it is vital to have it all in your plans.

Once you have developed the right mindset, you need to reevaluate yourself and your capabilities. Defining the scope of your operations and the limits are equally essential. But again, before you jump into starting an Amazon FBA business, think of the following:

Does the business fit your desired lifestyle? There is a difference between someone who spends two hours in business activities and another who spends ten hours in the same event.

In most cases, all the above mentioned want to be successful. What differentiates them is the drive for that success. If not taken seriously, you may end with a business structure that reflects what you don't like or did not expect. But when you take a step back and identify the steps needed to follow, you will find hat activities and processes are simplified and fit into your puzzle.

The Supplier vs. Product Approach

I believe that the right FBA mindset should direct you to find the supplier, not the product. Why so? The best business experience is defined by continuity; consistency. If you go shopping for the products, chances are you will find the products, but they may not be a good fit for the business. Let's say you walk into a casino and put all your money on the red chip of the roulette. What if the black chip comes up? The same applies to the FBA business. Risks are always there. Or perhaps the products are okay, and you sell so well, only to find it challenging to restock with the same product. You are done. You have to repeat the same processes of identifying the product once again.

On the other hand, if you can get a stable supplier that can offer a wide range of products, you can spread the working capital. You get a variety of products to choose from and have time to assess the ones that sell well and those that do not. You have the opportunity to invest in the right products and at the same time is assured that at no given point will you run out of stock. You can select related products to throw in the mix. This approach is more straightforward and lets you spread risk fairly. You can think about it in this perspective when a supplier requests a minimum purchase order of 100 units at $10 each, does it reflect spending $1000 on the supplier? My answer is no. Here you get a better deal compared to buying the same items at the same price from five different suppliers. How? The cost of shipping.

Go for What You Understand Better

I want you to figure out any retail outlet that will accept you as a good salesperson if you walked in on a vest and a tie. Or, did you start placing sodium in water, expecting a hissing sound for the first time in high school? Same way, can you identify an underserved market in your line of business? Can you look at a product and see the fault that you can expound on? It is not always about getting products from your suppliers and listing them on Amazon for sale. Go for the little unnoticed niches. Identify what you know best. It will help you improve and even innovate in areas other don't know. It gives a unique and competitive edge.

If you can notice a gap, fill it. If your competitors are offering a product at $10, but you can get the same product from a supplier that allows you to sell it at $8 and still make a profit, do it. After all, the best sellers on the Amazon FBA business model are those that establish a niche that they understand better.

Try Suppliers from Within the United States

Depending on the amount of capital at your disposal, you can get great deals from well-known brand names. I do not suppose you will get the Nike kind of products, but with the right presentation, you can find big players in the manufacturing industry offering you their products. Legitimate suppliers within the US industry are more reliable and easy to access for your stocks. I am not talking about the ease of shipment or the reduced costs only.

Knowing Your Customers

I have given you a step by step guide to honing your FBA mindset. If you follow the tips diligently, you will have higher chances of succeeding. All the same, the aim was to get you at the right starting point. Now I will take a look at the final space that you should occupy. Below are five essential mindsets that you are expected to possess if you consider the above tips.

1.   A Clear Understanding of Your "Why."

As an exceptional FBA seller, you know why you do what you do. It is almost similar to defining your success or identifying the purpose. And as they say, most leaders have a clear insight of what their firms do and even know how the processes are done, but great leaders are those that clearly understand why it has to be done, and the result afterward is the answer. A great mindset will let you know why you have to do what you intend to do. In the Amazon FBA business model, such a mindset will make you serve the customers with purposes and realize some decent income.

2.   The Right Mindset is to Help, Not to Sell

With the right FBA mindset, you need to understand the importance of the product to your customers. This way, you help them, as you trade. Quality-driven selling falls under this umbrella. You have to give your clients value for their money. This mindset will let you view your business as understanding your customers better, rather than a transactional entity.

3. Possessing a Clear Intent

The right FBA mindset is maintaining a clear intention to serve the customers in the best possible way. That is what makes the difference between manipulation and persuasion. If a customer finds out that the seller is all about sales, trust goes out the door. And believe clients are good at noticing it.

4. Focusing on What You Can Control

With FBA business, you can only control two aspects of your work; attitude and effort. Like I have said before, there will be challenges along the way, as is with most eCommerce businesses. The response towards the same makes the difference between a good seller and an average seller.

5. Listen More, Talk Less

The first essential aspect of service delivery is understanding the person you intend to serve. Customers may not point out their concerns directly. A smart seller thereby takes a lot of time to listen more in the course of making sales. You have to ask questions and engage the buyers lest you end up dealing with people you don't understand.

The most crucial first step is starting your business with the right mindset. It makes you a better salesperson and a better person in general. The best way to build a better mindset is by finding your central understanding with the customer.

Amazon FBA Selling Rules and Guidelines

Starting an Amazon FBA business comes with guided rules and regulations that govern the operations, ethics, and conduct of sellers. The FBA selling rules and guidelines are found on the Amazon seller central page. The following are Amazon's guided rules:

Selling Policies and Seller Code of Conduct

Amazon has set policies that govern how sellers conduct themselves when listing their products for sale. Sellers are expected to adhere to the rules to avoid being suspended from Amazon.

Code of Conducts for Sellers

This policy requires sellers to do their operations in a just, honest, and fair manner for a better selling and buying experience. The system requires sellers to uphold the following:

1.   Sellers are expected to disclose accurate information about their products to the buyers and Amazon at all times.

2.   Amazon requires FBA sellers to act justly and use the services and features provided to them without misuse.

3.   Sellers should not damage or abuse their peers or their products and ratings.

4.   Sellers are barred from influencing customers' ratings and reviews on their products.

5.   Sending unwanted information or inappropriately communicating with buyers is not allowed.

6.   Contact between sellers and buyers is limited to Amazon provided communication platforms.

7.   Sellers are not allowed to avoid the laid processes when conducting their FBA business.

8.   All selling operations on the Amazon account should be before Amazon authorization.

Failure to adhere to these codes of conduct may invite Amazon actions against a seller's account. The acts may include cancellation of listed products from the sellers' account, suspension of the account, suspending payment, or denial of privileges accorded to other sellers.

Accurate Information

Sellers are required to provide correct info about their listings. This applies to both Amazon and buyers. In case of changes, sellers must update their accounts accordingly and notify Amazon and their customers appropriately. For instance, sellers must provide their business names and brands correctly and list their products in the right category.

Acting Fairly

The policy requires all persons with an Amazon FBA business account to conduct their businesses lawfully and fairly and not misuse the services and features provided by Amazon. Amazon lists the following activities that fail to meet their fairness metrics:

1. Provision of information that is deemed misleading and inappropriate to both Amazon and the clients. Such actions may include the creation of offensive images or posting many details on the same product.

2. Manipulating the ranking of your sales or products, either through making fake orders or including false rank information in your product description.

3. Inflating prices after confirmation of an order.

4. Interfering with web traffic through bots or paid clicks.

5. Committing to damage the products and ratings of a competitor.

6. Giving permissions to third parties to act on your behalf in ways that violate initial agreements with Amazon or Amazon policies.

Ratings, Feedback, and Reviews

The policy that governs ratings and reviews lays down the dos and don'ts for sellers. Amazon gives strict guidelines to clients for the observance of relevant rules. An Amazon seller is not expected to influence the ratings of their products or pay for customer reviews and ratings. However, sellers are allowed to solicit feedback and reviews. Sellers are warned against:

1.   Paying or offering incentives to buyers to influence the ratings, reviews, and feedback,

2.   Requesting customers to remove negative reviews or encouraging customers only to provide good reviews.

3.   Requesting and encouraging customers who had a good experience with their products only.

4.   Rate or review their products or those of their competitors.

Communications

Sellers are not allowed to send unwanted or inappropriate information to their clients. All information is, however, expected to go through the seller-buyer messaging channel. The information provided is also limited to fulfill an order or enhance customer service. All communications that are meant for marketing through this channel are prohibited.

Customer Information

The information received from clients, such as contact information like emails, is meant to be used for the fulfillment of orders. Sellers are required to delete such contact information after the sales are completed and not to reach out to customers or share their data with third parties.

Circumventing the Sales Process

No party is allowed to go around the laid processes when conducting business on FBA. Sellers are not supposed to provide links that may divert customers to other websites or arrange for the transaction on other platforms other than Amazon or any other recommended third party.

Multiple Selling on Amazon Accounts

Sellers are only allowed to operate a single account. Additional, various selling through the account is not permitted. Particular circumstances may lead to being allowed to run other accounts. Amazon reserves all the rights to offer permissions for opening accounts and selling through the FBA channel. Merchants are encouraged to read more about the requirements to open and operate FBA business accounts.

Filing Notices of Breach and Violations as a Brand Agent or Agency

Amazon allows sellers to have agencies that protect their brands against infringements. This implies to owners of intellectual property, etc. the agencies and brand agents are permitted to act on behalf of the seller in submissions and contracts. On the contrary, active members with FBA accounts are not allowed to double as agents and agencies to other customers. Such individuals are not allowed to file infringement notices if the said notices are deemed to benefit their Amazon FBA selling accounts. The violation of this policy may lead to the termination of such a seller's account.

The rules and policies laid down by Amazon are meant to establish smooth business processes and avoid unlawful and unfair competition among sellers. The codes of conduct are aimed at improving ethical practices that ensure customers are served effectively, and they receive value for their money. Sellers are advised to take note of these regulations to avoid putting their FBA seller account into risks of termination.

Chapter 3: Features of Amazon FBA

Amazon FBA business model offers a variety of benefits to sellers and buyers alike. The model provides many programs designed to suit business owners and their customers in several ways. A seller is allowed to outsource various operations like management of products, customer service, and fulfillment of orders. A prime member FBA business owner is given free two-day shipping while the rest get free shipping for spending more than $25. One of the features that benefit buyers is the Subscribe and save feature, which allows them to reap discount rewards for placing recurring automatic orders.

Management and Fulfillment of Inventory

The best part of using Amazon FBA is that it takes storage, packing, and shipping responsibilities off the shoulders of the seller. With the Amazon FBA business design, sellers don't interact with customers directly, when sales are concerned, because Amazon takes over the management of the products once they are shipped to the fulfillment centers. This is an essential feature that makes FBA sand out from the rest of the eCommerce business models.

Prime Shipping

One of the most popular shipping features of the Amazon FBA business model is the prime shipping. The feature allows prime members free two-day shipping. For non-prime subscribers, other shipping features allow free shipment for eligible goods. The feature might not be as fast as those of prime members.

Sellers are advised to look for the prime logo that is prominently featured on FBA products to benefit from this feature. It has been established that more than 85 million prime subscribers received discounted offers on top products and shipments for using FBA. Additionally, buyers are encouraged to purchase prime products making prime sellers more revenue compared to the non-prime products.

An additional shipping feature is an offer for free shipping for orders over $25 to all buyers. The only caution to take is making sure that the products are eligible for this offer. The list of these eligible products is available in FBA. Other features that offer such incentives are Amazon coupon deals and specific buyer programs such as Prime and Cyber days. All products listed on FBA qualify for such offers.

Higher Search Ranking

A feature that gives products listed on FBA an edge over other products on Amazon is the more top search ranking. The program allows all FBA products to get a high ranking on Amazon search results. In essence, when a customer searches for products on Amazon, the algorithm is set to pop up FBA products first. This leads to a higher ranking of all FBA products, thus increased sales, and revenue to sellers.

Multichannel Fulfillment

Amazon FBA business model fulfills orders for sellers who use multiple channels and online marketplaces like eBay to make their sales. This feature is called a multi-channel fulfillment (MCF). Under the function, the storage fee charged for inventories remain the same, while the multi-channel fulfillment fees are slightly higher than the standard fulfillment fee. The MCF fees range from $2.2 to $143.3 for every unit plus an additional 92 cents for every extra pound.

The MCF feature allows sellers to choose various shipment methods for their products. The shipment methods available for MCF are standard shipping, expedited two-day shipment, and priority one-day shipment method. The variety of shipment options is beneficial to sellers who offer the same though their other selling platforms. The MCF shipping rates are also lower compared to personal shipping rates.

The point to note is that all MFC shipping rates only apply to products sold on your website or other marketplaces other than Amazon. The same feature does not attract

Amazon seller fees. The cost of storage levied for such products is the same as products listed on FBA and takes the same seasonal changes in prices.

Small and Light

The small and light feature offers reduced costs of fulfillment on certain products. The feature is designed to give sellers an extra profit margin. As it infers, the offer applies to small and light items of 10 ounces and below. The products have to fast selling to qualify for this feature. Additional features that are eligible products for this offer are; they must cost less than $7 and with a volume of less than 16*9*4 inches.

The feature allows for a reduction of between 80 cents and a dollar for every unit ordered. Additionally, weight handling of 11 cents and packing of 75 cents are applicable. With the cheaper FBA fees, this feature is a perfect fit for sellers who want to test foreign markets. Combined with prime subscription, the feature allows beginners to try their luck in international trade, in which products are shipped within five days instead of the usual two days.

Subscribe and Save

This is a feature for buyers. The subscribe and save feature on the FBA business model gives buyers rebates and reduced or free shipping when they subscribe to certain products. The feature provides clients steady deliveries at the intervals of their choice. It also improves sales by giving sellers recurring customers. Apart from benefitting buyers, the program also offers sellers steady revenue. Additionally, the feature does not levy an extra cost to sellers who invite clients to subscribe to their products. The only requirements are for sellers to meet set minimum ratings of 4.7 on Amazon and have a good product standing.

Amazon Partnered Carrier Program

The Amazon partnered feature allows sellers to access shipping services from Amazon's carrier partners at a reduced cost. The program also allows FBA business owners to ship as little as a single order.

Customer Service Provision

FBA business model offers customer service to buyers on behalf of sellers. The feature allows sellers to concentrate on other issues affecting the business. Services offered are customer queries response and overall dealing with the buyers.

Global Selling

Amazon is the most important online market place in the world. This allows sellers to access customers worldwide and expand their business beyond national boundaries.

Automated Unfulfillable Removals

This is considered the best feature for sellers with a wide variety of products. It is evident that some products will sell slowly and needs to be removed and disposed of to avoid the accumulation of storage fee. This feature allows such sellers to subscribe to their products to be removed from fulfillment centers after a period of not selling. The products are automatically deleted after a lapse of this period.

Other Special Features

Email Notifications

One of the requirements, when one is opening an Amazon FBA account, is providing a business email that ca be used to contact the seller about updates and notifications. Through the email notification feature, FBA can send notifications to your customers as well. The additional feature to this one is the notification email cc. This allows sellers to add their email to be CC'd when Amazon sends notifications to customers.

To benefit from this feature, go to the checkout data link found in the upper right corner of the order page. Alternatively, you can add the email automatically by using the applicable rule that filters orders with such links. The law should state, NOTIFICATION EMAILSC|EMAIL-ADDRESS. To auto-add your email, you replace it with the rule.

Marketplace ID

The marketplace ID feature allows sellers to attach their identity to orders shipped to customers from other countries. FBA sends the ID automatically. Sellers can also add a different marketplace ID for different orders by setting checkout data known as MARKETPLACE_ID and replacing and replacing the field with their ID of choice. When this field is left unfilled, Amazon does not send any ID along with the order.

Declared Value

Under the feature, a seller is required to state the value of the listed product in the same currency as the fulfillment center receiving the inventory. This is done through the filling of the FBA order form. The money may differ from the original transaction currency. This feature is specifically designed to serve seller trading across borders and is essential in adjusting accounts for exchange rates.

Amazon FBA Tools and Providers

The Amazon FBA business model provides a plethora of third-party tools to help sellers in managing. The tools range from return calculators to research tools. The variety of tools is meant to help sellers run their business smoothly. As much as Amazon has inbuilt training and support tools for FBA business owns, third party tools are equally important to consider. These tools simplify the processes involved in setting up and running the FBA business. Each provider of these functional tools has different features and avail them at ranging prices. The most used third-party tolls in FBA are:

Sellics

This product is designed explicitly for FBA business owners, merchants, and agencies. The tool offers assistance in analyzing products, tracking revenues and profit ratios, and helping sellers manage their pay per click advertisement campaigns. Sellics come I a full suite package that is most suitable for creating and running a professional FBA account. The software starts for free and costs up to $257 per month (payable annually), depending on specs.

Inventory Lab

This essential research tool helps sellers with keyword searches, product analysis, competition research, and product listing. The software is used in managing products, sales, feedbacks, and customer comments on the product. Inventory Lab can also be used for Amazon advertisement campaign management. Beginners and established sellers on Amazon FBA can use this tool to improve their FBA businesses. The web-based software starts at free and costs up to $899 per month, depending on the volume of sales.

Jungle Scout

As the name suggests, the jungle scout is research software. FBA sellers cab scout for new products in the market, track the sales of the product and receive analyzed estimates for sales data. I general, the tool is designed to make product research easier and simpler. With the software, seller receive automated system for email follow-ups and product listing builder on Amazon. The software costs between $39 and $419 per month.

Ship Bob

The web-based software, Ship Bob, allows sellers to move products from Shabbos warehouses to Amazon fulfillment centers. The tool prepares orders that have FBA label and other processes. In short, the device is designed to help a seller with other logistics allowing them to focus on other essential business operations.

How Fulfillment by Amazon Works

Amazon has two fulfillment options for sellers. The fulfillment by Amazon (FBA) and merchant fulfillment network (MFN). In MFN, sellers are allowed to handle all order fulfillment and shipping processes. In FBA, the procedures are taken care of by Amazon. When a customer places an order on your products, Amazon checks the closest fulfillment center to the client, picks, packs, and ships the product to the buyer on behalf of the seller. Furthermore, tracking information is given to the customer directly from Amazon, and within two working days, their order is delivered (in the case of prime membership).

With fulfillment by the Amazon business model, a seller is required to ship his or her products to the nearest Amazon fulfillment centers for storage as they wait to be sold. The products can be sent to the Amazon storage facilities directly from the supplier, provided the due procedures are followed. Sellers can also use tools like ShipBob to store the products or ship the goods to the Amazon fulfillment facilities. The scheduled processes for storing inventory in one of Amazon's fulfillment centers are explained in other chapters of this book.

Amazon handles all inquiries from customers, including product refunds and returns. This system allows sellers to be in business but has little responsibility for running the business.

Who FBA Business is Right For

The Fulfillment by Amazon business model is suitable for all eCommerce sellers without personal storage facilities. Additionally, if you don't want to manage the products directly, offer customer service, and other related tasks, you may find FBA just the right eCommerce model for you. Nevertheless, some business is more suitable for Amazon FBA than others. Here we take a look at the businesses and people that perform better with Amazon FBA.

FBA works well for entrepreneurs in general. People who take their time to fine-tune their products to spread better profit margins find FBA an impressive selling point. Amazon rules selling rules change rapidly, and it makes this kind of people to change the product s and inventories to be in line with the requirements, processes, and procedures. FBA works better for people who commit their efforts and resources to start small to grow and expand in the long-haul.

Another group the fits well with Amazon is the eCommerce retail store owners. With the knowledge of eCommerce business, these sellers find transitioning to FBA easier. Additionally, seasoned merchants can attract more clients when they change to selling on Amazon. The platforms may be different, but the idea is almost the same, with some slight changes in rules and regulations.

Merchants with already existing brands and products may also find FBA a better selling place. The marketplace requires sellers to list products for sale. If product research is done wrong, the seller may find their products taking longer to sell. On the other hand, readymade brand names are popular, and customers usually go for them. Such businesses find it easy to navigate Amazon selling.

Using the FBA business model to sell your products can be an excellent opportunity to earn some decent income and get a lot of insight on how to navigate the continually changing eCommerce business environment. I would advise potential sellers and first-time merchants to consider the steps and guidelines laid in this book to assess whether starting and operating an Amazon FBA business would be a smart move for them. Evaluating the costs involved in setting up FBA business pitting against projected income is equally important before you dive into this business.

In some cases, the cost of involved with FBA business may be higher compared to running an eCommerce business through personal websites, depending on the products you intend to sell. For such scenarios, it is advisable to go for the cheaper options that guarantee profits, such as the MFN. Alternatively, you can opt to use other eCommerce marketplaces like eBay to build your brand first before you move to Amazon FBA.

Chapter 4: Pricing Strategy

Once you have the complete product listing in your Amazon FBA business, you need to identify the best pricing strategy. If the products are available in bulk, you will also need to keep a repricing tool in mind to help you keep your prices as competitive as possible and ensure good profit margins. A lot of factors are considered when coming up with the right price for your products. The investment put into the product, and the forces of demand and supply are essential in determining the right price for your listed products.

This chapter takes a look at the available pricing strategies that sellers can use to maximize sales and profit margins. Amazon pricing strategies can be utilized manually or automatically.

Very High or Very Low Prices

If your prices are too high, you will be left with your stock as sellers go for your competitors' products. On the other hand, if you price your product too low, customers will scramble for your products at the expense of profits. It is, therefore, essential to strike a balance between the two to keep the customers happy and still reap some functional benefit. If you are a seller and would like to establish the midpoint price, here is how:

Do Not Present the Lowest Price in the Market

The assumption is always that customers will flock your products if you have the lowest prices. The answer is yes; clients will scramble for your products. But all this comes at a cost. First, you may end up making losses. Another possibility is that the clients won't last long. With time they will perceive your products as an inferior quality, which may drag you to the bottom of the ranking table. The best recommendation is getting yourself somewhere around 1.5% to 2% above the lowest seller. By doing this, you find yourself competitive enough and avoid getting caught among the worst-ranked. Alternatively, you can set your minimum selling price at 25% to 30% above the cost and fess involved in purchasing and listing the product. This essentially means that you are projecting your profits by about 25% to 35%. You can adjust the prices according to seasons and other market factors.

Flow with Your Peers

If you do not want to apply the above strategy to establish your prices, you can follow this one. Check out what your competitors are charging and match their prices. If the prices vary in the same category, you can go for the highest and the lowest rates then get the average of the two. This means that you are neither the cheapest nor the most expensive.

This strategy is perceived as the most aggressive and useful pricing tool. You are neither risking losses nor cultivating doubts in your customers. The result is increased sales, which lead to better product ranking and reviews. In cases of slow-moving products, you can adjust the prices (repricing) by setting a floor price for the goods. In considering your competitors to establish your rates, watch out for shrewd sellers who engage in undercutting and other activities that would hurt your profit margins.

Use Your Intelligence and Experience to Determine the Price

The best part about Amazon FBA business is that your experience and knowledge is always put to the test. In pricing, you can use the two to determine which price is suitable for your products. This can be done through the following.

1. Projecting the future by using previous data. You can study past trends to predict what will likely happen next. This way, you stay ahead of the pack and can adjust your prices accordingly.

2. Watching out for your competitors' moves. In a highly competitive environment, you should treat your business as a game of chess. Study your opponent, know their movements, and stay ahead.

3. Evaluating your products to know what needs a slight boost to sell and what is a completely lost cause that should be sold as fast as possible.

4. Data is an essential tool in any business operation. Embrace it. Use consumer data to make predictions.

Identify Specific Items for Repricing

It is essential to go through your inventory to identify the orders that need to be repriced before you avail the entire pack for the final sale. For instance, slow-moving products that stay mostly in the FBA warehouse than in the hands of buyers should be checked first to avoid having an old stock. Alternatively, you can start at the top of your pricing formula. Go for the highest-priced items then reduce the price by a certain margin. Buyers who had initially seen the price will get a little excited by the knocked off-price prompting them to buy, thus increasing your sales volume.

Apply the Supply and Demand Principles by the Use of Software

The best strategy to use for repricing is studying the forces of supply and demand. If the items on the shelves exceed what buyers would ask for, there are chances that customers will tend to hold off such products for a while until their prices go down; do the necessary. Conversely, if the demand for a particular product eclipses its availability, buyers will be rushing to get their hands on the product; give it a little price boost for increased profit.

Amazon has repricing tools like RepricerExpress, which allows sellers to automatically compare their prices with those of its competitors in the same category. The software can also be used to adjust prices accordingly by setting the floor price and the maximum price within which a product should be sold. Another factor that influences product prices is the visibility of the product in search ranking and the performances of sales of the product on Amazon.

The two factors require that a seller adjusts the prices to reflect the position of the product compared to its peers in the market. Going through the process manually is usually not viable, especially if the inventory at your disposal is so huge in units. Sellers are increasingly relying on the repricing software to adjust their prices to remain competitive in the market. The shift in technology and other business factors makes the incorporation of such pricing tools an essential part of Amazon FBA business and the eCommerce industry at large.

When repricing is considered, it is worth noting that the software and other tools for repricing are only tools as they are called. This means that the final decision should rest on the seller's shoulders to identify which prices to compare and with who to compare. The decision to reprice should be in line with the objectives of the business and the long-term targets of the seller.

It is essential to understand that there are merchants in the FBA business framework dealing in the same line of products. In the same way, you should note that they are entirely different businesses with varying abilities, objectives, and product listings. Using them to compare your prices should come at well thought and analyzed circumstances on the ground. Using a repricing tool to give solutions to modern pricing strategies is essential and provides a seller with the ability to fix their prices according to the need of the business.

Why Pricing Matters

When you finally get to launch your first product and list it on Amazon, you get swayed by a lot of aspects to consider in the product. You think about the size, the color, the packaging, and so on. All these come about due to the need to make your inventory highly marketable and competitive in the market, as much as the FBA business model is concerned. Of all the factors that ring into your mind, there is one that is very critical and should worry you more in the launching stage and throughout the business life; the price of the product. The prices you stamp on your products are a significant influence on the ability of the product to sell or remain a sitter (spend more time in the warehouse than in the hands of buyers). Prices influence sales in two ways:

1. Appraisals determine the amount of profit you receive

If the prices you levy on products is way below the recommended market price, chances are you will be making no profits. Or perhaps you may end up losing so much on sales. On the other hand, if the prices are high, you make a lot of money, leading to higher profit margins.

2. Prices determine the amount of stock you sell

Pricing is essential in determining the volume of sales. If the prices are low, buyers will flock the products, leading to increased sales volume. Conversely, if the prices are high, clients will be put off, leading to a low amount of sales.

The two ways in which prices impact your business performance works together in a complicated and risky approach. As a seller, you have to determine the amount that is just high enough to give you maximum profits and low enough to avoid losing customers to your competitors. Striking a balance is essential in coming up with an equilibrium price that works both for the benefit of the clients and the business.

3. The fee charged for the storage of products

There is a third in which prices may influence the profits you make as an FBA seller, and that is through the Amazon storage fees. If the products are priced highly, they will not attract customers hence ending in the warehouses for an extended period. Amazon charges sellers a monthly storage fee depending on the season. Additionally, there is an extra storage fee charged for products that sit in the fulfillment centers for more than 365 days. If you are not careful enough, the prices may end up eating into your profits.

As can be seen, price is a fundamental and essential factor that needs to be got right. The process of coming up with an equilibrium price is not a one-time exercise. Pricing needs to be done regularly through monitoring and researching the trends in the market and the competitors. Regular price adjustments are also critical in remaining relevant in the market.

Pricing Strategies That Are Based on the FBA Business Model

When considering pricing strategies and sourcing advice from various people on the same, it is crucial to take into account the models that best suit your situation and are in line with the objectives and targets of the business. Most importantly, you should plan to implement a strategy that goes well with the model of business you are operating and the types of products you are selling. Many strategies can be used to price private label products and inventories under the umbrella of wholesale or retail arbitrage model. All the procedures used have different implications for the business.

Strategies to Price Products That Fall Under Wholesale and Retail Arbitrage

When your business is dealing with items through the wholesale or retail arbitrage model, you have to note that you are not just competing with the same products but also other merchants for the buy box. The price of a product is one of the most crucial factors that Amazon considers when determining who to award the buy box for a given item. This means the prices you stamp on your items have to be very competitive for a chance to be considered ahead of your peers in the FBA business.

FBA sellers are advised to keep a close eye on the Amazon seller central to utilize the available resources in beating the competition and identifying opportunities to maintain equilibrium price. The seller central has many original features that can be used by sellers to adjust their prices accordingly. Such features include the pricing dashboard and manage to price. Additionally, the Amazon seller central also gives s pricing suggestions to sellers. FBA merchants can access this useful tool through the *Report Tab* and clicking on the *Amazon Selling Coach* before proceeding to choose *Pricing Options* found under the reports.

Another critical thing to note when pricing within this model is that you should maintain your prices so that you do not become the cheapest seller in the market. As much as this might win you the competition, it might also lead to being ranked among the bottom performers, not mentioning a hit that it will have on your profit margins.

Pricing Strategies for Private Label Products

When dealing with a private label product in your FBA business, you become the only seller offering the product on Amazon. This means that you do not compete with other sellers to win the buy box or your products. The most challenging aspect of this is that you have to come up with a pricing strategy that is competitive compared with other sellers in the same category. The effect of pricing in a private label model moves from influencing the sales and profits to the reputation of the entire brand. If you go for the lowest price, clients might consider your brand "cheap." On the other hand, if you are the most expensive, customers will go for other alternatives.

With private label products, sellers need to price-with-value. This is to means that if your product has an additional feature that lacks in your competitors, you can go for an extra dollar. Buyers will acknowledge the distinctive features of your brand even if the price is slightly higher than your competitors. This reflects the value and high quality to buyers, something they don't shy of spending on.

Depending on the type of products you are offering, it is crucial to look out for the features that capture the buyers' attention. If something is lacking in the outcomes of your competitors, try to design your items to have it. Find a solution to the complaints of your competitors' customers. This way, you will have an easy time justifying your prices, and clients will see no harm in spending an extra dollar on your brand.

Quality Speaks for Itself, but Let the Buyers Get the Message

The most important way to express quality is by having positive reviews on your products. The problem with this system is that customers tend to leave reviews, mostly when they have a terrible experience with the product than when they are satisfied. It should be your concern to create a system that makes it easier for your clients to leave reviews and give you feedback. You can solicit reviews through emails or creating a quick link for your customers to use.

How to Manage to Reprice

Sellers that find themselves competing for the buy box must identify ways of regularly adjusting their prices to stay relevant in the market. The process of assessing and improving product prices to fit prevailing market changes is called repricing. From a practical viewpoint, sellers usually have a variety of options to consider when managing their adjusted prices.

Repricing Manually

Under this strategy, sellers have to check the prevailing factors such as their competitors and adjust their prices accordingly. This practice is best suited for merchants who offer a small volume of inventory, which gives them enough time to check the progress and trends of their competitors manually.

Using Software to Reprice

Another approach that a seller can take in repricing is using repricing tools. The software monitors what your competitors are charging and adjusts your prices accordingly. The software considers the information and guidelines you provide to research and improve your rates. This approach is suitable for sellers with large volumes of inventory.

Automated Pricing Through the Amazon Seller Central

The last option for adjusting prices is using the Amazon seller central price guide. This feature works in the same manner as the repricing software. It uses information from other sellers in the same category and offering the same products to adjust your prices accordingly. You can also set the limits within which you want your prices to be modified.

Final Thoughts

Prices play a significant role in the success of the Amazon FBA business. It is, therefore, vital to invest a lot of time and research I determining the best pricing strategy that suits the business. It is advisable not to devalue your products so much that your prices end up dragging you down. On the other hand, it is equally important not to be swayed by greed to overprice your products and in the process, end up losing your clients to your competitors. Finding the equilibrium price that reflects the value and quality of your products and at the same time goes well with the clients is essential.

It is worth noting that no recommended strategy can work for all sellers in a given situation. FBA merchants must consider their businesses separately and discuss approaches that best suit their goals and ambitions and reflects the actual value of their brand.

Amazon FBA Fee Structure and Cost

The costs involved in starting an Amazon FBA business include monthly fees that are charged from the end of the first month of registration, shipment costs, product costs, and the cost levied on third-party tools. Sellers using FBA also pay for monthly fulfillment and storage costs. It is crucial to research to ensure that the products you are listing are fast selling because these costs can accumulate at some points leading to losses. Here is a breakdown of the costs involved in starting and running a fulfillment by Amazon business:

Monthly Subscription Fees

For a professional seller account, you will be required to pay a monthly fee of $39.99 payable per month. For an individual account, you do not have to pay any monthly subscription fee. Instead, an individual seller account owner pays 99 cents for every item sold.

Additionally, individual seller account attracts 45 cents to $1.35 selling fee for every unit listed. For a serious starter, it is advisable to go for a professional account that attracts a lot of benefits from Amazon. Otherwise, for someone trying to test the waters, an individual account is not wrong.

The Cost of Fulfillment

Amazon will charge you for picking your products, packing the goods, the shipment cost, and handling customer services on your behalf. The return for these costs starts at $2.41 for every unit listed. Alternatively, a seller can be charged $137.32 for particular items. The unique items are determined according to size and weight. If the inventory goes beyond a specific size or weight, it is considered unique.

Stock Removal and Disposal Fee

Sometimes you will find out that a particular line of goods is not selling or selling slowly, leading to accumulations of storage fees. For these reasons, there is a need to dispose of the stock to get working capital. To remove this stock for disposal, Amazon charges a fee of $0.5 to $0.6 for every unit you intend to discard. This cost can be avoided by

conducting proper market research on fast-moving goods.

The Cost of Labeling

As indicated in the section of how Amazon FBA works, there are strict guidelines and barcodes for label specifications for the products shipped to Amazon fulfillment centers. If a seller fails to follow the instructions and stock is found to be mislabeled, they will be charged a labeling fee of $0.2 for every unit with a wrong label.

The Costs of FBA Preparation Service & FBA Unplanned Product Preparation Service

Amazon's FBA business model provides strict product packaging and preparation guidelines. Sellers are required to prepare their products well for listing and sale before they are shipped to Amazon fulfillment centers. If you fill like the guidelines and regulations are too much for you, you can have the intervention of Amazon to prepare and pack the products for you at a fee. On the other hand, if you ship the products to

Amazon warehouses and they are found to be ready and packed improperly, you will be charged an unplanned prep fee. The cost of these services varies according to the type and features of the products in question. The initial payment starts at one dollar to about $2.2 for every unit of goods.

The Cost of Processing Returns

Amazon does not charge a seller for processing necessary returns in most of the categories. However, for classes with free customer returns, Amazon FBA charges a fee that is equal to the initial fulfillment fee. If the product needs to be repackaged for sale, Amazon will charge a repackaging fee. The repackaging fee is, however, not disclosed.

The Cost of Storing Products

Amazon charges a seller for storing products at one of the Amazon fulfillment centers. The cost of such storage varies with size and weight. Additional storage cost is also levied on goods that stay in the warehouse for long without selling. The storage cost starts at 48 cents per unit (cubic foot of space covered) to $2.4 for every cubic foot. This cost also varies according to seasons.

Long-Term Storage Fees

This is the additional cost levied on goods that stay in the Amazon Fulfillment Center for more than one year (365 days). The fee charged is $6.9 per cubic foot of space held in the warehouse or 15 cents for every unit. Whichever of the two charges is greater is used.

The Cost of Shipping Products to Buyers

Amazon FBA takes the responsibility of delivering products to customers from the seller. However, the seller is required to pay a shipping fee for this service. The cost of shipment varies with the carrier used. Amazon negotiates with its partnered carriers to give their customers a discounted offer while shipping their goods to clients.

Additional Amazon FBA Fee Structure and Cost

When starting and operating an Amazon FBA business, a seller needs to consider some costs involved that do not come directly from Amazon. These costs can come from product purchases or other third-party tools that are used to make selling on Amazon easier. Sellers can ship products from online marketplaces like Alibaba, which has thousands of goods to offer on wholesale at the cost of as low as under $10. In most cases, Alibaba offers a minimum order unit of 100 units.

Amazon's FBA tools that help in the smooth running of business include Sellics, InventoryLab, and JungleScout. These third-party tools help manage FBA business, conducting research, and many more. The cost of using these tools range from free to around $100 per month.

The Cost of Storage on Amazon FBA by Season

The table below indicates the fee charged by Amazon for storage according to seasons.

Season	Standard	Oversize
Jan - Sep	69 cents per cubic foot	48 cents per cubic foot
Oct - Dec	$2.40 per cubic foot	$1.20 per cubic foot

The table above indicates that the cost of storage is increased for the season between October and December. For a beginner, you need to take note of this period. You can avoid using Amazon for storing your goods between these periods to reduce the expenses involved in your business operations.

Chapter 5: Sales and Marketing Strategy

Preparing Your Products for Sales

Step Five: Launch Your Brand

The process of launching your product can be taken care of in the previous phases of setting up the FBA business. But since you will have to be patient as the first consignment of your product is shipped and prepared for sale, you will have to sit down and establish a brand for your business. Several guidelines can help in creating a unique and perceptible brand that will identify you with the products that you offer.

Giving Your Brand an Identity

At this point, you have narrowed down to the exact product that you will offer in your FBA business. When it comes to giving your brand identity or simply naming your brand, you will need to broaden your view and imagine how you would like your business to look in the coming years. You need to consider the products that you would wish to add to the existing line when your business has grown. Once you have established how your business will be structured and known the products to add in the future, you can now come up with a brand name that encompasses all these features.

You can consider putting down a list of brand names that fit your business model in the long run and are in line with what you intend to accomplish. Secondly, you need to research to find out if other businesses are already using the names you have chosen. This step is essential to avoid using a brand name that is already in use, which will portray your business as a counterfeit. Brand names that have domains should be considered. This makes it easy for you to register the domain when setting up a website. Consider a brand name that clicks all the above boxes. The graphic quality of the name is also crucial because it helps in creating a logo for your brand.

Creating a Brand Logo

Designing a logo for your brand will depend on the brand name that you have chosen. If you have knowledge about graphic design, you can as well do it on your own. If not, then you need to seek the help of an artist with the same. Make it simple and avoid too many details to reduce the cost of designing the logo. A simple logo is often apparent when scaled to a smaller size compared to a logo with too many intricacies.

Creating Brand Themes and Tag-lines

Apart from having a brand name and logo, you will need to create a theme and tag-lies that identifies with the product to make it exceptional and distinguishable. An eye-catching idea or motto for your brand can go a long in selling the product. Make the sentence short but on point to reflect the product. Make sure that your theme brings out various concepts that are related to the product, the brand name, and are appealing. You need to think from a broader perspective when coming up with a tag-line that will help develop your identity and personality in the market and mirrors the message that your products send to the clients.

Copyright Your Brand Name and Logo

Dedicating a lot of time and resources in creating a brand name and logo is a sure way of starting a limited liability company. For this purpose, you need to have the brand name and logo registered. Your unique feature should count as intellectual property to avoid copyrights. To register your intellectual property, visit the U.S. Patent and Trademark Office website, and follow the steps.

Step Six: Create Your Product Listings

You have reached a point where your products are ready and your identity established. The next vital step is preparing to list your products. Here, you will need to put in more focus and innovative and creative measures. You have initiated a lot of plans to have your products with FBA. You need to make sure that you create a listing that not only attracts your clients but also give them a lot of insight about the product to help them make rational buying decisions. A good product listing is among the significant factors that affect the level of revenue you get from your FBA business. Below are steps to help you create a reputable product listing.

Proficient Snapshots of the Products

You need to take stunning photos that show various features of your products. You need to communicate the importance of the product to your customers through the gallery. Product photos of low quality will destroy the reputation of the business and all the hard work and resources that you have put in place. When listing your products, the attached photo should communicate the value of the product to the customers adequately and reflect the resources you have put together to come up with the product. At times, your supplier may provide product photos when shipping the items. If not, you need to hire a reputable photographer to get you some.

Comprehensive Product Titles

The title of your product is the only element of the product that will attract the attention of the customer searching for products on Amazon. Be sure to include some unique, simple to understand descriptions to your product title to attract the attention of budding buyers towards products. To come up with the best product title, you should research leading products in your category to see how the listing is done. Evaluate the claims, noting those that are exaggerated and avoiding them. Settle on what you feel is essential.

Write Your Product Descriptions

The description of your product should be concise and easy to read. At the same time, you need to ensure that the descriptions offer enough information about the product to help your customers make sound buying decisions. To do this, here are some tips to help you generate product descriptions that will boost your sales.

Define the ideal buyer in a familiar and detailed tone. This step is similar to creating a good character in a play. Know the background of your perfect buyer. Consider their professions and income level. Find out where they live, what they like, their personality, etc. In general, you should identify your ideal buyer and get more insight into the buyer. The knowledge of the customer is essential in determining how they would like your product. Clients always exhibit the same buying patterns. If you can find out what they look for in a product, you can come up with a description that attracts them to your products.

Conduct a market study. Go around, checking the descriptions of other sellers within your category or related categories. Analyze what you see, noting the approaches that sound appealing, and salable. Create an outline or a template that combines the best descriptions in different styles and tones. Use the templates to generate your product description.

Generate your most appealing tone. Use an informative, professional, friendly, and conversational tone to describe your product. The sound should be comfortable for you and the customers. Let a friend review the tone for corrections.

Make use of incredibly sensory words that stimulate human imaginations. Such words can be derived from action verbs. Avoid sticking to everyday language and maintaining a somber tone. Make it light to appeal. Additionally, alter the beginning of paragraphs or numbered list with words that are unique and highly sensitive to avoid being mind-numbing and predictable. Lastly, in the use of language, make sure to capture striking features of the products, such as the benefits accrued from using the product.

Anticipate possible queries that your clients may have and their concerns towards the product you can create a list of "most asked questions about the product" and give an answer for each. This step is made possible if you know your ideal clients. The questions and answers should be included in the product description.

Generate the final product description in short, easy to read sentences. Include titles in the description. Communicate every essential aspect of the product in a summarized paragraph. This summary will help your customers to skim through the description, noting the vital features they would like to get from the said product. The product description should give an overview of the product in general.

Now that you have a product description, you will need to fill in the relevant areas in Amazon's FBA product description form. The form is set up to provide crucial information about the product to help the buyers know what they are purchasing. Indicate the color, size, dimension of the product, weight, and information about the warranty if applicable, guidelines for installation, and many more specs. This information is essential in making informed buying. The information you provide about the product will determine whether a customer chooses your item or those of your competitors. With all that in place, you proceed to the final step.

Marketing with Ads
Step Seven: Marketing Your Product

There is a chance that your products will sell if the listing is right, appealing, and professional. This is because Amazon is the largest online market around the globe, and listing your products, there is a guaranteed selling chance. However, the sale will be in low volume and incidental. To start selling your product in a way that guarantees satisfying income, you will have to grab the attention off the potential buyers. The truth is that you will have to advertise your product I ways that make it stand out from the rest of your competitors'. Do you want to get started? Here are some tips to help you go about the process.

Pay Per Click Advertising

As a newbie in the industry, you will not have the necessary resources to go the Madison Avenue way. You need to start small and hope to adjust to more prominent platforms for advertising your business. Make use of simple and affordable methods of advertising. One of the cheapest and easiest methods to announce your business is through pay per click forum (PPC). PPC offers an affordable and straightforward way to attract the attention of potential clients. In a nutshell, PPC is a sponsored content that comes up when you search the many search engines.

When a person is going through the search results and decide to click on the link that leads them to your product, you are obligated to pay the PPC Company a particular fee according to your agreements. The advantage of using this method to advertise your product is that you can keep track of every penny you spend on it, knowing that it reflects the promotion of the product. You can advance your game by using PPC linked to more prominent companies that offer products in your category to reach even broader market segments. This way opens your product to certified buyers that may lead to more significant profit margins.

Use Advertisement Platforms like Jump Send

Jump Send is a very convenient advertisement tool that ensures you get more audience. The device further guarantees better organic standing on Amazon and gives your products added appraisals. JumpSend assists you with establishing cut rates, gifts, and tokens as well as managing automated email promotions. The platform allows sellers to access more than one hundred thousand customers in their network. The access improves the sales and increases the standings for various keywords on Amazon that are of interest to you.

Prompt Lots of Reviews for Your Products

Some clients may not be used to your products and wish to try them for the first time. To remove their doubts about the goods, they will tend to go for reviews and ratings of your products. The opinion of other buyers about your product can go a long in persuading other buyers who do not know about your product to buy it. The reviews and ratings of your products are an excellent way to increase sales. Potential buyers will always want to see the experience of other people who are using your products. Apart from just encouraging buyers to post reviews about your product, you can go ahead and invite them to try the products and post reviews if they feel satisfied. You can also offer gifts and discounts to customers who give your product reviews. The more reviews your products have, the more they attract potential customers.

Make Good Use of Social Media

The majority of people, including your potential customers, spend most of their time on social media platforms. You should use this as an opportunity to reach out by marketing your products through social media. Marketing on social media platforms gives your products a professional look. The products can also be shared among friends, which gives your products an additional market reach. You can create a page for your brand or share them through your timeline. Here are some tips to help you set up an excellent social media marketing strategy.

Pick one at a time. Draw your focus on one site first. Avoid chasing your tail. Chances are, if you work on all social media platforms, you are bound to be ineffective. Pick one channel to put all your attention. Once you have built a good base and you start seeing returns, move to another channel, and work diligently.

Set up a page for your brand. Make the page fun, engaging, and interactive as possible. Invite people to like, engage, share, and comment on your brand. You are likely to get more buyers if your interaction with customers is superb. Keep the conversation going by inviting questions and giving answers and more information about the products you offer.

Use influencers to promote your brand. Get to involve reputable people with massive followers in promoting your brand. Social media influencers can help advertise your brand to greater success. Give them some gifts to engage with your brand and share them with their followers. If possible, ask them to rate and review your products.

Pay to advertise on social media. Social media can offer a cost-effective advertising platform for your business. This comes about due to the ability to direct your advertisement to an exclusive audience and groups of interest.

You can target a section of qualified customers, drawing their attention towards your products. Eligible customers are usually buying customers, which makes your sales rocket high. Bear in mind that advertising on social media can be inconsistent. The pattern of use of these platforms changes from time to time. Be sure to use it as a supplement rather than your entire operation base. Shift to channels with the greater pull of users and change your marketing strategies accordingly. You don't need to put all your eggs in one basket.

Blogging, Vblogging, and Podcasting

In the concluding section of this chapter, I will advise you to hold off on this idea for various reasons. Anyway, if you are launching your brand on a larger scale, then you will need to make the right moves in your marketing strategies. This type of content marketing should be in line with your business targets, objectives, and long-term dimensions, although the use of these forms of media varies, and your execution will have to be flexible enough to contain the dynamism. Make use of the following tips to optimize your product advertising strategy

Restructure the content of your posts to relate to the products you offer, the use of the products, added information, and a parallel comparison to competing brands in the same category as yours. Optimize the use of your content, making it as informative as possible. You can consider paying experts to do the work for you. In making comparisons with other products, avoid diminishing the value of your competitors, instead show how powerful your product is compared to the rest.

Link your content to other providers and websites. The main objective is to make use of their followers. This idea is similar to using influencers on social media. Content providers with a vast follower base will attract potential buyers to your products and brand. The more they interact with your brand, the more chances of increased sales.

Consistency is vital. You don't want people to interact in your blog only for you to disappear the following day. Hummer, your followers with a purpose, regularly, and avoid nonsense in your posts. Maintain reliable content, with useful and informative guides about your products. Consistent interactions laced with a sense of purpose, and construed content analysis will do you the tricks.

The content of your post should be informative, not all about sales. Purpose of serving the interest of your followers and watching them help yours. If you are all about making sales, they may be driven away from your posts. Engage your audience, focusing on a single purpose at a time. Ask for opinions on how to improve their user experience.

Buildup Your Email List

You should harness the power of email subscribers to get your Amazon FBA business off and running. This form of product promotion does not substitute targeted email marketing, and rather, it's a supplement to the same. Create an email list of your customers. These are people who have used your products and endorsed the same. How do you get them? Creating a link on your posts inviting them to subscribe to email notifications. Here is a closer look at this essential marketing tool.

The first thing to note is that your subscribers are equally important and valuable as your sales. These are people who have approved your brands. Treat them as you would treat your sales. You need to form such kind of an attitude when creating an email list. Why the emphasis? These are sure customers. They are more valuable than potential customers because they give a foundation to your customer base. These are people you can rely on when your sales are dwindling or when you have a new product on the market. They love you and your brand.

You need to encourage people to subscribe to your email notifications. Create invitations, promotions, and incentive programs to get people to subscribe. Be very active in soliciting for subscriptions. Do not let that email list rot. Give updates and notifications regularly. Consider offering discounts to these buyers (for purchases over a fixed period) and announce new stock. The more subscribers you get, the more successful your FBA business gets.

The content of your emails should be similar to those of your website. As discussed earlier, customize the content to reflect the interest of the subscribers. It is never about sales all the time. Give useful updates and information about products, guiding your audience on use and tips rather than striving to feed your greed.

Use Coupons and Special Deals

You have probably come across products listed with two prices, a lower price above a higher rate that is crossed. The purpose of this is to draw the attention of buyers to the product. Everyone likes an incentive or a discount. Take note of Black Friday sales. People scramble for such deals. This is the point, coupons and exclusive deals are tested methods of improving sales. Make use of Amazon tools or bargain hunter and promotional websites to advertise your products. The more people you can get your hands on, the more likely you will boost your sales. An additional tip on this is, a slight discount that attracts more sales is more valuable than fewer sales at the original price.

Additional Special Tips for Your FBA E-Commerce Marketing Strategy

The steps laid out above are fundamental in establishing your FBA business and growing it for a decent income. The tips and guides provided offer foundational principles to not only help you in getting started in the Amazon FBA business model but also grow your business. If you follow the steps, you are sure to succeed in the venture. But why stop there? You need some extra tips, especially if you are eyeing a more established business in the future.

Follow that passion. Consider pursuing a line that you are most passionate about. Passion will make you wake up early every morning to advance your business. You will not get bored with constant update requirements, research, and more study about the brand you offer. If you are not feeling it, you will not dedicate more time to it.

Strive to grow. Every successful business owner offers more to the market. Once your startup has found some ground, upgrade, add more products, and improve the business further. You do not want to be in the same position five years from now, do you?

Improve your Amazon bestseller ranking. Beating competition is a sure way of staying relevant for a very long time. The success of your business depends on it. Even though the BSR may not be a measure of your progress, improving the same attracts more customers and promotes your sales.

With the right course of action, your brand can become a household name. Remember how we discussed the themes and tag-lines of established businesses in step five? Use the same tactics to create an easily recognizable brand that reflects your identity to the market. Your sites should be accessible to sight.

Become an Amazon affiliate. Do you want a win/win situation for you and your host? Refer more people to use Amazon. You will not only earn a commission from Amazon from this but also get a potential customer who may end up buying your products. Is there any other better way of doing business?

If you have been paying attention to the tips, steps, and guides provide, you will realize that most of the first words used in each paragraph infer the mind-bender word "POISE." Do you know why? Studies have shown that it takes self-assurance to start a business from scratch and grow it successfully. When done in the right way, your FBA business is "poised" to make you a decent income.

Summing Everything Up

The Amazon FBA business model is structured to utilize the gods of Amazon in providing storage and other fulfillment functions to make your business simple and work easy. The advantages accrued from this model makes it possible to start a business and earn some decent income depending on resources that pump into the business, be it time or money. The venture provides a good side hustle that grows to replace your primary job. In that sense, it offers a chance to work at home.

In a nutshell, this chapter has been a continuation of the first chapter and has offered guides to set up your Amazon FBA business. The seven essential steps (continued from section one) provides a basic outline to establish an FBA venture. When done in a focused and purposeful way, the steps are fundamental I launching a highly profitable business. There are additional tools and plenty of resources that can help you with the same. However, this book provides the basics in simple language and easy to follow guides.

Strive to be more informed in the field and motivate yourself to start small and grow. However, in so doing, you need to take caution to avoid a bad start that can be discouraging or lead to a plunge. Beware, and here is how:

Hold off setting up a new blog or website if you are just getting started. The idea is getting started. At this stage, you need to minimize expenses and avoid the complicated process. Make it simple, easy, and cost-effective. When establishing your brand, you were advised to create a functional theme and name with the available domain. This implied that at some point, you would want to set up a website or a blog for product marketing purposes. That is only applicable in the long run once your business is up and running.

For a start, you need to dedicate your time and money elsewhere. In content marketing, you are required to spend a lot of time producing posts that are attractive to customers and investing some right amount of money on the same. How about you skip this step and come back to it when you are all geared up? You have bigger fish to fry. You need to keep your business moving instead of being slowed down with such processes.

Starting a Private Label

Private label products are goods that are specifically manufactured by one company for sale by another separate firm under a different brand. The most widely known individual label products are Amazon Essentials, Great Value Brand, and Mainstays.

Finding Private Label Products

Private label products boast a lucrative niche for new sellers in the Amazon's Fulfilled-by-Amazon (FBA) program. Finding the right private label is easy, and many tools can help FBA merchants in identifying private labels to help drive the success of their business. The steps listed below help identify and create a private label that can generate more income for your FBA business.

1. Brainstorm Product Ideas that Fit Your Niche

Ideas can be sourced from any sphere of life. There are plenty of hacks that can generate appropriate ideas for private label products. The first way of identifying an idea is by looking out for new trends. Trendy products are those that your nearest retailer or wholesaler is yet to stock. You can be the first to get your hands on the products and sell them through Amazon's FBA.

Another place to hack top ideas is Amazon. Go through the departments one at a time. Look at the subcategories for hot new products taking note of the *Hot New Releases* sections. Brainstorm what other fellow sellers have in their Amazon storefronts ad product listings. Alternatively, you can take google for smart ideas. The internet has a lot to offer. Social media platforms are also hot places to find what innovative individuals have to offer.

2. Look at the Specific Features of the Products

If you are just getting started, it is recommended that you go for products with particular characteristics and qualities. Some of the qualities you can look for are:

Small and light. The best private label products for starters should be small in size and light in weight. This idea is to help the merchant save on shipping costs.

Avoid seasonal products. The products you sell should not depend on seasons. Products like Christmas gifts, winter clothing, etc. are not great for a starting business. You need something that can sustain the business in the long run.

Products with no regulation are the best. Go for products that do not have red tape. Unregulated products are usually natural to manufacture and distribute.

Look for simple products. There is a lot of fun in selling products that do not give you a lot of headaches in handling or dealing with customer queries all the time.

3. Do Extensive Product Research

If you have identified some excellent products that you feel will fit the market niche you want to exploit, take time to conduct more research on the products. Find out more about the product, what can be improved, and what is not suitable for sales.

4. Conduct Supplier and Manufacturer Research

You have the perfect product in mind. The next step is figuring out where you can get the products. Research the market to find the right supplier or manufacturer who can stock your business with the product. Identifying a supplier is essential in establishing a steady flow of products.

5. Do Your Product Logos, Design, and Packaging

A private label product allows you to design your logo and make it your brand. You can create your logo or let graphic artists do it for you. Additionally, you can customize the products to have your preferred look. Customization can be done by changing the color of the product or the package.

6. Determine Your Fulfillment Strategy

Identifying the product and the right supplier is just halfway through the business journey. The other half is identifying the fulfillment strategies for the products. You have to decide the channels of fulfilling your orders. The most reliable fulfillment service is Amazon's FBA.

7. Create Your Product Listing

Take time to create your product listing. Following the Amazon guidelines, gather the necessary materials to create your final product listing for your Amazon FBA business. The next step after establishing your product supplier determined your fulfillment strategy, and created an excellent product listing is placing your first order and shipping the products. You can choose to send the products to yourself or have them shipped to one of Amazon's fulfillment centers. The latter is the more cost-effective of the two options. If you decide to have the goods shipped to Amazon fulfillment centers, then you have to follow the specified Amazon guidelines on how to prepare and ship your inventories.

Chapter 6: Essential Facts and Skills for Amazon FBA Business Owners

Amazon is by far the largest online marketplace in the world. Like any other market, Amazon has its rules and regulations that control operations in and within the business model. Additionally, the Amazon FBA business model has a unique combination of information and skills that an FBA business owner and sellers need to master to enhance the growth of their businesses for a satisfying income. This chapter takes a look at these basics that should be considered for better FBA business operations. The section also summarizes the book in the conclusion segment to offer a brief overview of what is required, done, and how it is done to establish and grow a successful Amazon FBA business.

The following are basic knowledge that a seller should have at fingertips to succeed in the eCommerce industry.

1. Purposeful Marketing Strategy to Build Product Listing and Boost Product Sales

If the products that you intend to offer are already available from other sellers, this step may not be of the essence to you. The inference is down to the fact that, in such circumstances, you are only required to provide necessary pricing information, the quantity of the merchandise, and the SKU name information. In terms of the listing, you will only add your products to the already existing product listings.

But if the products you intend to offer are unique and new to the Amazon inventory list, you will be required to come up with information to fill up various slots. The slots include the title of the products, product description, brand name, the logo of your brand, and may more as discussed in the book. To find out if your product is new, you can search the product in the Amazon catalog by feeding in the keywords that describe your products. Product photos are also essential for listing. For more information on how to add a picture of your product, check out the Amazon's adding images support page. Sellers are encouraged to have multiple photos of high quality to attract clients.

2. How Well Do You Understand Your Product Sourcing Avenues?

This point cannot be stressed less. Customers will not wait for you to find more products to restock. They will opt for products from your competitors, and chances are you may lose them forever unless they are your friends and family. Either way, you will lose a substantial sale amount and income. You need to stay on top of your game. If your products sell fast on Amazon, you have to find faster ways of replenishing your stock. The need calls for a well-established supply channel, which improves your sale rates and cash position.

3. Do You Want to Stick to One Product or Plan to Add More Related Items to Your Stock?

The decision lies solely with the seller. If you plan to sell one item all through, then you can take advantage of Amazon's restocking notifications tools available in the seller central. Alternatively, you can use various prediction tools that show the market patterns, changes in demand, and supply units. These tools also offer multichannel inventory order management.

If the long-term plan is to add more products to your brand, you have to identify the products, conduct market analysis, and launch them at the right time. This line of business is highly recommended for growth purposes.

4. Establishing Processes to Identify Products

Everyone wants to sell their products as fast as possible. Well, the reality on the ground is that some inventory doesn't sell. They need to be liquidated soon enough to help into their conversion into working capital. Amazon has a lot of tools that can be used to identify products. FBA business owners are meant to benefit from such research tools. Alternatively, you can monitor inventories through the SKU to identify the goods that need to be cleared. For the best Amazon FBA business experience, sellers need to know which products are fast going and which ones are selling slowly. This helps in saving additional storage costs.

5. Understanding the Amazon FBA Cost Structure

Many sellers on Amazon have the fundamental insight of the SKU-level profitability. The knowledge of this cost structure only gives an overview of the sellers' profit level, but fail to indicate the drivers behind the profits and their percentage contribution towards the profit. This way, they fail to understand the products that bear money expenses and cost to sell on the Amazon FBA business model.

In the same case, sellers fail to know their profits and revenue until the end of the official financial year, when the accountants give the final financial report. A seller needs to assess and compile all the overhead costs and integrate them into the cost of operation and other expenses. This approach helps in the computation of profits and losses.

Learning from Competitors

6. Identifying Your Competitors in the Market

It is essential to know who is selling the same product you intend to avail of to the market. Many first-timers find it challenging to cope with the competition because they listed products without identifying the competitors and the level of competition in that category. Before you list your products on Amazon, strongly recommend that you carry out a study to spot check their intended listing against the Amazon fab catalog. Well, unless you want to rub shoulders with the big boys, in which case there are higher chances that you will lose.

If highly accepted household brand names already list the products that you intend to sell, you should walk away. The same applies to prices. Always gauge the price points that are mostly accepted by consumers. If the product you ae listing is priced so low by other sellers, beware that you may end up not selling much at your price.

7. Determining the Time Needed to List Products After Registration

How long do you have to wait after registration on Amazon FBA before you start listing your products? On the same note, the processes involved should be at your fingertips. Amazon does not levy charges on newcomers until the end of the first month. Within this period, you are required to follow due processes of creating product offers and activating some suggestions with a sellable inventory. The longer you take to list products, the more you get charged for doing nothing. Once your seller account is active, you will be charged monthly, whether you sell or not. So, sit down and make actionable plans to get you moving in the first thirty days.

The final step in doing business is identifying the feeling of your customers about your product. The same applies to Amazon FBA business. Amazon uses sales feedback to gauge the performance of your business. As a new seller, you have to identify methods of getting feedback from your clients to help assess your business. Many tools can help you in seeking customer feedback such as Feedbackgenius.com, Salesbacker.com, Bqool.com, and many more. All these tools can help you solicit a response from your buyers and share their experience with your products. Alternatively, you can invite your customers to leave comments, reviews, and ratings every time they make purchases.

Conclusion

This section is entirely based on customer experience to help first time sellers understand the Amazon FBA business environment and serve their customers better. The part summarizes the book offering more insight into what buyers look for in a seller. It is designed in question-answer format, reviewing the most asked questions about FBA business, and giving accurate answers to help you wade through the same without glitches.

These are most asked questions about Amazon FBA business

What does FBA stand for?

As indicated earlier, FBA is an abbreviation that stands for **"fulfillment by Amazon."**

What is the Amazon FBA business model?

Amazon FBA model is a business form that allows sellers to leverage the vast fulfillment networks by Amazon. In using the business model, sellers are entitled to Amazon storage facilities, which fulfills their orders and provide customer care services on their behalf as well. In essence, sellers are made to look like any other business entity without spending much effort into their products. All you have to do is list products and let Amazon take care of the business for you.

What benefits does a seller get from using Amazon FBA?

The challenge that faces most eCommerce business models in navigating the logistics of fulfilling orders and distributing products to the clients in a good time. However, Amazon FBA lets you utilize their fulfillment program to take the challenge off your shoulders.

Another complication involved with an eCommerce business is the problem of storing products and keeping track of the inventory as well as listing products. With the Amazon

FBA business model, sellers only have to ship their products to the nearest Amazon fulfillment center and let Amazon taken care of the rest.

The two benefits alleviate two of the most confronting challenges that sellers in an eCommerce business model face. This allows their businesses to grow, and for the following reasons:

1.   Sellers are made free to focus their efforts and resources on other essential business operations like marketing, developing new products and brands, and conversion rate optimization (CRO).

2.   Amazon offers a variety of incentives that the seller and the customers can benefit from. Such perks include; customer care services, free shipments, quick delivery of goods, handling credit cards, etc.

3.   The FBA business model designed to support the growth of your business. Amazon lets you focus on other business essentials rather than chasing orders.

4.   Reduced costs of operation. The shipment of products and orders are made more comfortable and affordable compared to using private e-business facilities.

How much income can a seller get from an FBA business?

Well, to be sincere, this is a tough one. Many determinants influence the amount of revenue generated by an eCommerce business, FBA included. I cannot offer any typical results. However, starting an FBA business can have an explosive income potential if done right. Following the steps and guides provided in this book is a sure way to get started and earn a handsome income. In essence, there are possibilities of earning up to seven-figure income if you utilize the FBA business model and leverage the power of Amazon well.

Assessing the business

The table below can be used to evaluate the readiness of the business from an operational standpoint to start selling on Amazon.

Problem statement	Yes	No
Do you have good marketing content that can be used to build product listing?		
Do you have a clear understanding of your product sourcing avenue? (That is, if your products are selling fast, do you have proper channels to replenish the stock fast enough to avoid long periods of stockout?)		
Are you planning to sell the same product throughout or intend to introduce a new product once your business is established?		
Do you have a proper channel for identifying products that are not selling fast and need to be liquidated?		
Do you understand the Amazon cost structure?		
Do you know who is selling the same product you intend to list on Amazon? And do they sell well?		
Do you know the time needed to start listing your products after registration? If yes, do you understand the process?		

If your answers to these questions are yes, then you are ready to get started.

The Amazon FBA business model offers a lucrative opportunity to potential sellers in the eCommerce business sector. If done right, the venture can turn out to be a very handsome income generator for many beginners and established merchants alike. However, there are substantial risks that can threaten the growth of FBA business, especially if proper guidelines are not taken into consideration. Amazon lays various rules, directions, and policies to help the sellers navigate the processes and have a good seller experience, and services offered to FBA sellers are designed to give opportunities to sellers to utilize Amazon's vast customer base and fulfillment channels. By taking care of most business activities and operations, Amazon lets merchants free to focus on other important aspects of their business that may impact better profits through higher sales.

The Amazon FBA business model is by far the best eCommerce platform for sellers looking for a decent side income or a full-time job. The purpose of this book is setting a foundation for anyone hoping to start an Amazon FBA selling business. This is a guide on the necessary steps, the dos, and the don'ts to make it easier for beginners to get into the business. Further research on the same is highly recommended. If you are just getting started or already have experience in Amazon's FBA, it is important to take time to advance your knowledge. My final thoughts are; whatever you decide to do, follow your instincts, and identify what really works for you.

What most people find challenging in an eCommerce business model is the process of inventorying added products. However, the FBA prototype allows you to ship your inventory to Amazon warehouses and let them take over the rest of the operations from there. The process of setting up your business, however, requires some step by step analysis and guides to ensure that you are eligible to get started. This book offers the best guidelines for getting started in fulfillment by Amazon.

www.ingramcontent.com/pod-product-compliance
Lightning Source LLC
Chambersburg PA
CBHW070317240526
45467CB00045B/535